Baseball!

Q&A

Smithsonian | Collins
An Imprint of HarperCollinsPublishers

BOSTON

Smithsonian Mission Statement

For more than 160 years, the Smithsonian has remained true to its mission, "the increase and diffusion of knowledge." Today the Smithsonian is not only the world's largest provider of museum experiences supported by authoritative scholarship in science, history, and the arts but also an international leader in scientific research and exploration. The Smithsonian offers the world a picture of America, and America a picture of the world.

Special thanks to the National Museum of American History, Behring Center, Smithsonian Institution, for their invaluable contribution to this book.

Special thanks to Ted Spencer, Vice President and Chief Curator, National Baseball Hall of Fame, for his invaluable contribution to this book.

This book was created by **jacob packaged goods LLC** (www.jpgglobal.com)
Written by: Gary Drevitch
Creative: Ellen Jacob, Jeff Chandler, Carolyn Jackson

Photo credits: **pages 4, 5:** The Corey R. Shanus Collection; **page 37, inset:** The Penny Marshall Collection; **page 40:** The Sears Collection; **pages 1, 2, 8, 10, 11, 12 (both), 14, 17, 22, 24, 27, 29, 31, 32, 33, 41, 42:** APImages; all others: National Baseball Hall of Fame Library.

 For information address HarperCollins Children's Books, a division of HarperCollins Publishers, 1350 Avenue of the Americas, New York, NY 10019. www.harpercollinschildrens.com Library of Congress Cataloging-in-Publication Data Baseball! : Q&A / Smithsonian Institution. — 1st ed. p. cm. ISBN-10: 0-06-089947-6 (trade bdg.) — ISBN-13: 978-0-06-089947-9 (trade bdg.) ISBN-10: 0-06-089946-8 (pbk.) — ISBN-13: 978-0-06-089946-2 (pbk.) 1. Baseball—History. 2. Baseball—Miscellanea. I. Smithsonian Institution. GV862.5.B36 2007 2006017795 796.357—dc22 1 2 3 4 5 6 7 8 9 10 ❖ First Edition

Contents

The Brooklyn Atlantics, shown here in an 1868 trading card, were the hottest team in baseball during the 1860s.

How did the sport of baseball get started?

The sport we play today started as a game called rounders. Young men and children began playing it in England in the 1600s. Rounders players hit a ball with a bat and ran around bases to score, just like in baseball. But there were some big differences. In rounders, when a ball was hit to a fielder, he threw it *at* the runner. If the ball hit the runner, he was out, or "soaked."

What were the first organized baseball teams?

English colonists brought rounders with them when they came to America. But by the early 1800s, some people started calling it "baseball." For many years, fans believed, incorrectly, that Abner Doubleday invented baseball in Cooperstown, New York, in 1839. But we now know that in 1845, Alexander Cartwright of New York City wrote the first baseball rules. He also started the first club that played by those rules—the Knickerbocker Base Ball Club. Cartwright's rules got rid of soaking. Instead, runners had to be tagged out by fielders. His rules also said that the first team with 21 runs at the end of any **inning** won the game. Today's rule that the team with more runs after nine innings wins came along in 1857.

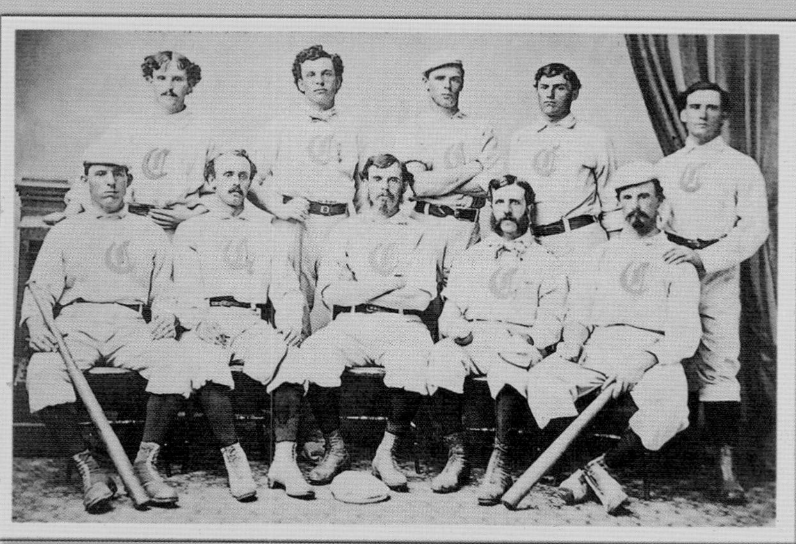

The Cincinnati Red Stockings won all 65 games they played in 1869. The next year, they won another 27 straight games before the Brooklyn Atlantics ended their streak.

What are the oldest major-league teams?

The owners of eight baseball teams came together in 1876 to start the National League of Professional Baseball Clubs. All the players in the league were paid. The teams agreed to play a 70-game season, but some teams could not stay in business until the end. The Chicago White Stockings had the league's best record (52–14) and were the first National League champions.

That team is still playing but is now called the Chicago Cubs. The only other original National League team still playing is the Boston Red Caps. But the Red Caps moved out of Boston long ago. We know them today as the Atlanta Braves.

The 1876 championship Chicago White Stockings team appeared in the *Chicago Tribune Magazine.*

How many major-league teams are there?

Today, there are 30 teams—14 in the American League and 16 in the National League.

AMERICAN LEAGUE

- Los Angeles Angels of Anaheim
- Oakland Athletics
- Toronto Blue Jays
- Tampa Bay Devil Rays
- Cleveland Indians
- Seattle Mariners
- Baltimore Orioles
- Texas Rangers
- Boston Red Sox
- Kansas City Royals
- Detroit Tigers
- Minnesota Twins
- Chicago White Sox
- New York Yankees

NATIONAL LEAGUE

- Houston Astros
- Atlanta Braves
- Milwaukee Brewers
- St. Louis Cardinals
- Chicago Cubs
- Arizona Diamondbacks
- Los Angeles Dodgers
- San Francisco Giants
- Florida Marlins
- New York Mets
- Washington Nationals
- San Diego Padres
- Philadelphia Phillies
- Pittsburgh Pirates
- Cincinnati Reds
- Colorado Rockies

Each of the 30 major-league teams sends at least one player to the All-Star Game each year.

Ballplayers spend a lot of time in the **dugout** during the long 162-game season.

How long is a baseball season?

The better the team, the longer its season will last. Every team begins its season in February, with spring training and exhibition games to help get ready for the new season. Around April 1, the regular season begins, and it lasts 162 games, ending around October 1. If a team makes it all the way to the World Series, its players could play in as many as 19 more playoff games. For the best teams, a season could last more than eight months.

There are **25** active players on a major-league team's roster, which increases to **40** active players on September 1.

Only **four teams** from each league **make the playoffs.**

Are all baseball parks the same?

No two ballparks are exactly alike or exactly the same size. Some have unique features—like the 37-foot left field wall in Boston's Fenway Park.

Everyone calls it the Green Monster.

Baseball's rules, however, require some things to be the same wherever the game is played. The pitcher's mound has to be 60 feet 6 inches from home plate. Each base has to be 90 feet away from the next base.

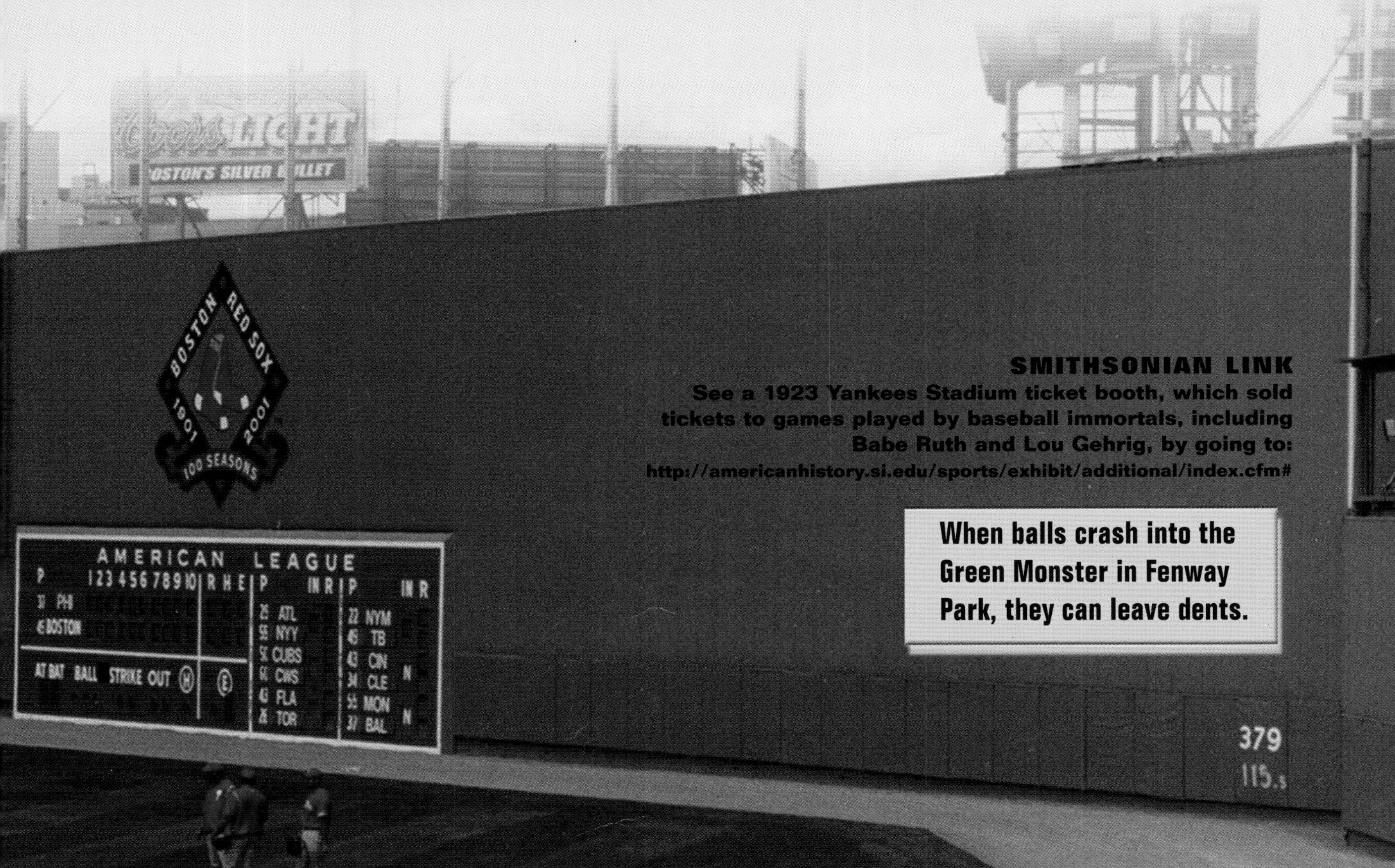

SMITHSONIAN LINK
See a 1923 Yankees Stadium ticket booth, which sold tickets to games played by baseball immortals, including Babe Ruth and Lou Gehrig, by going to:
http://americanhistory.si.edu/sports/exhibit/additional/index.cfm#

When balls crash into the Green Monster in Fenway Park, they can leave dents.

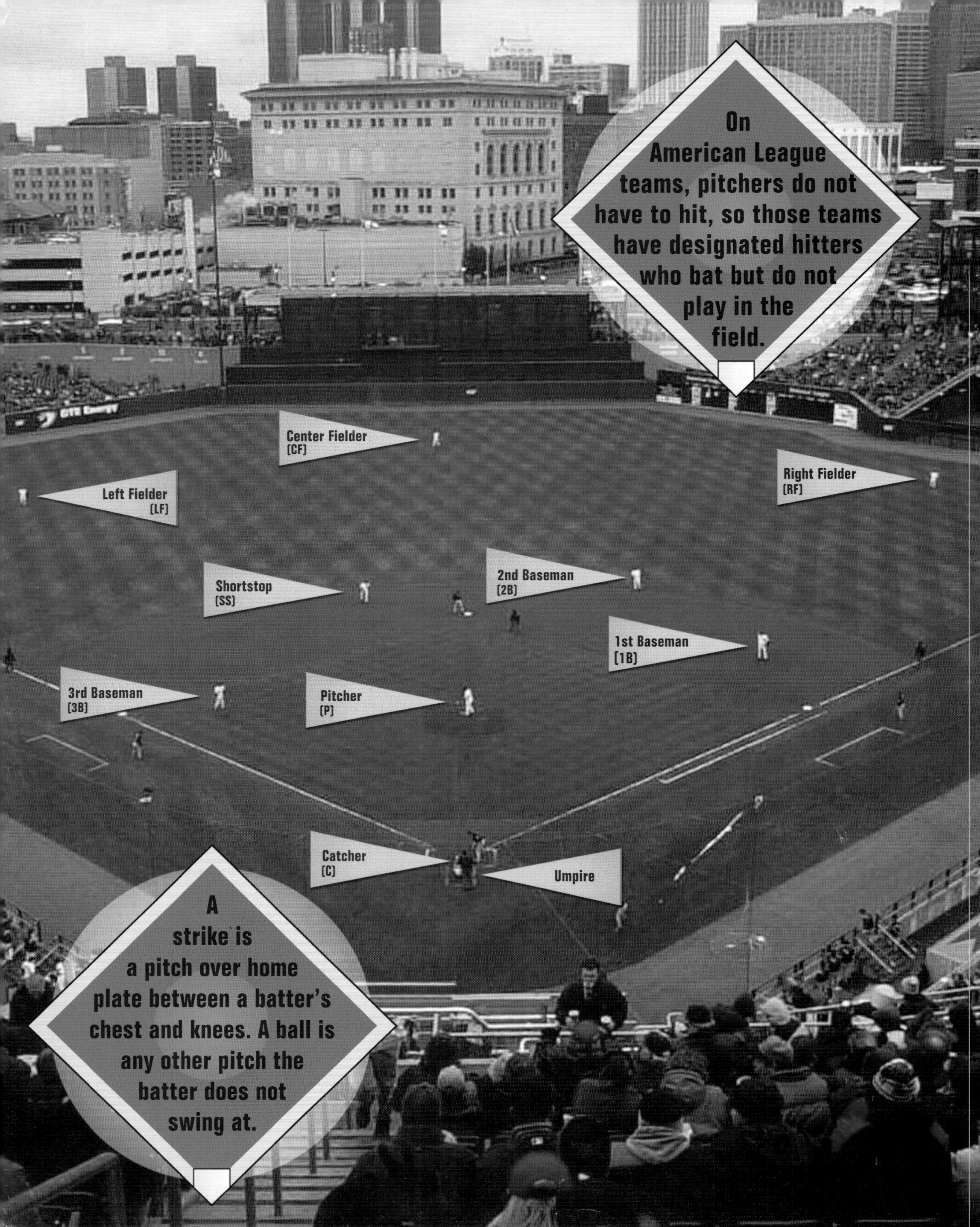
On American League teams, pitchers do not have to hit, so those teams have designated hitters who bat but do not play in the field.
Center Fielder
[CF]
Left Fielder
[LF]
Right Fielder
[RF]
Shortstop
[SS]
2nd Baseman
[2B]
1st Baseman
[1B]
3rd Baseman
[3B]
Pitcher
[P]
Catcher
[C]
Umpire
A strike is a pitch over home plate between a batter's chest and knees. A ball is any other pitch the batter does not swing at.

What are the positions on every team?

When a player comes to bat, nine fielders from the other team are spread out across the field to try to keep him from scoring. There are three outfielders—one each in left, center, and right field—and four infielders—a first baseman, a second baseman, a third baseman, and a shortstop. The pitcher stands on the pitcher's mound and throws to the catcher, who squats behind home plate.

Is it a ball or a strike?

Even if a batter doesn't swing at a pitch, he can make an out or get on base. When a batter swings and misses, it's called a strike. If he doesn't swing, the umpire standing behind home plate decides if the pitch was a strike or a ball.

Three strikes—either swinging or called by the umpire—make an out. Four balls make a walk, and the batter goes to first base. Any ball hit outside the playing field is a foul ball. A foul ball counts as a strike, but it cannot be a third strike. If a batter already has two strikes, foul balls don't count.

If a player argues with an umpire's decision, the ump can throw him out of the game.

Bartolo Colon, one of baseball's hardest throwers, won the 2005 AL Cy Young Award.

How fast is a fastball?

Several pitchers can throw a ball as fast as 100 miles an hour, daring batters to swing hard enough to hit it. Players call the fastball "the heater," "gas," or "cheese." The best fastball throwers, like Mariano Rivera of the New York Yankees and Bartolo Colon of the Los Angeles Angels of Anaheim, use different grips and motions to make their pitches rise or sink as they approach home plate.

Knuckleballer Tim Wakefield shows how he holds his unusual pitch.

The **knuckleball** is one of the hardest pitches to throw because of its unusual grip—and because it's hard to control where the pitch is going.

Sandy Koufax struck out more than 300 hitters in a season three times.

Does a curveball really curve?

A good curve, or "the hook," is one of the hardest pitches to hit. Curveball pitchers use a special grip and snap their wrist downward as they throw. This makes the ball drop as it reaches home plate. Los Angeles Dodgers legend Sandy Koufax had one of the best curveballs of all time. Batters said it looked like it was falling off a table, and few ever figured out how to hit it.

SMITHSONIAN LINK
See Hall of Famer Sandy Koufax's glove and a list of career accomplishments by going to:
http://americanhistory.si.edu/sports/exhibit/gamemakers/koufax/index.cfm

Knowing how to slide into a base is important for any ballplayer. Alex Rodriguez was safe on this play.

How do batters get on base?

The object of the game is to score runs, but you can't score unless you get on base. Batters can get on base by getting a hit or collecting a walk, or if a fielder makes an error trying to catch or throw the ball. The most painful way to get to first base is to be hit by a pitch. Craig Biggio of the Houston Astros should know. He has been hit by a pitch more often than any player in history—273 times by the end of the 2005 season.

What's a stolen base?

As a pitcher begins his throw, a player on base can try to run to the next base. If the runner reaches the base before he's tagged out, then he's stolen a base.

In 1982, Oakland A's outfielder Rickey Henderson set a record with 130 stolen bases. Detroit Tigers star Ty Cobb stole home an amazing 54 times in his career.

Only three players have stolen more bases than Ty Cobb, who swiped 892.

Why do baseball players wear numbers?

The numbers help fans tell the players apart. In 1929, the Cleveland Indians and the New York Yankees were the first teams to put numbers on the backs of their jerseys. The Yankees assigned numbers based on the batting order. Babe Ruth batted third, so he got number three. Lou Gehrig batted next, so he got number four. After they retired from baseball, the Yankees "retired" both their numbers. That means no other Yankee will ever wear them again. Today, all players wear numbers, and most teams put each player's last name on the back of his jersey.

When did fielders start using gloves?

In baseball's early days, players didn't wear gloves. They fielded balls with their bare hands, and it usually hurt. Some players began wearing gloves around 1870, and by 1896 they all did. Back then, players left their gloves on the field to be shared with players on the other team. Major-league players were still allowed to leave gloves on the field between innings until 1954.

SMITHSONIAN LINK
See the catcher's mask Steve Nicosia wore while catching Game Seven of the 1979 World Series as a rookie for the Pittsburgh Pirates by going to: http://americanhistory.si.edu/sports/exhibit/additional/index.cfm#

When players come to bat, they wear hard plastic helmets. Batting helmets had been around since the 1940s, but players were not required to wear them until 1971.

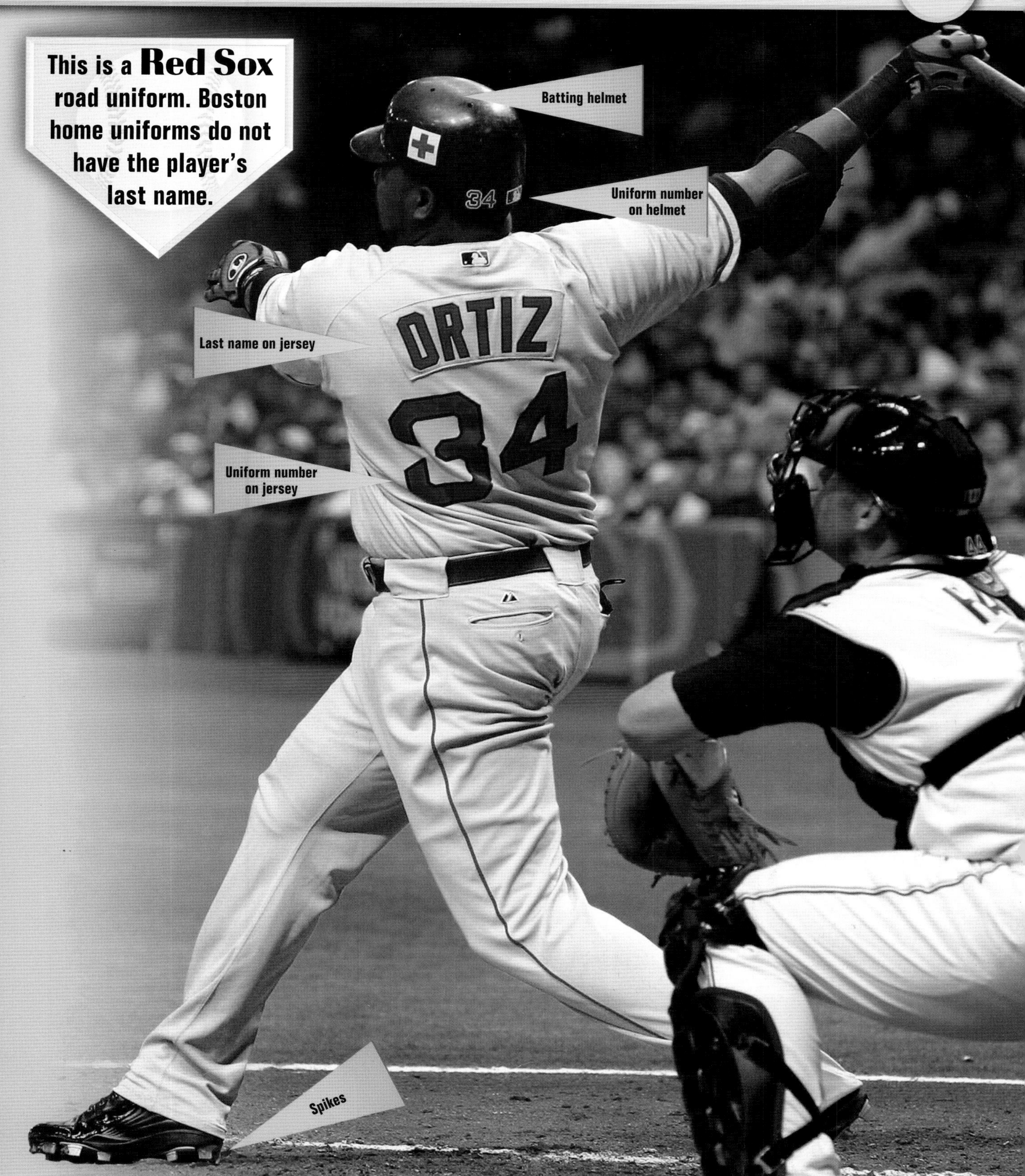
This is a Red Sox road uniform. Boston home uniforms do not have the player's last name.
Batting helmet
Uniform number on helmet
Last name on jersey
ORTIZ
34
Uniform number on jersey
Spikes

Ted Williams was not just a great hitter, he was also a fighter pilot and a champion fisherman.

Ty Cobb is one of only two players with more than 4,000 hits. He had 4,189.

Who are the greatest hitters of all time?

A player's batting average is his number of hits divided by his number of times **at bat**. Three hits in ten at bats makes for a great average of .300. Boston Red Sox outfielder Ted Williams was nicknamed "the Splendid Splinter" and wanted fans to remember him as "the greatest hitter who ever lived."

He is the last player to hit higher than .400 in a season.

He hit .406 in 1941. Detroit Tigers legend Ty Cobb had the highest career average of any player, .367.

Who are the greatest fielders of all time?

Third baseman Brooks Robinson of the Baltimore Orioles won 16 Gold Gloves between 1960 and 1975.

Fans called him "the Human Vacuum Cleaner" because he scooped up any ball hit his way.

Shortstop Ozzie Smith won the award 13 times. "The Wizard of Oz" was also a favorite of fans for his habit of doing a backflip as he ran onto the field.

Every season, each league gives **Gold Glove** awards to the best fielders at each position.

With Brooks Robinson at third base, the Baltimore Orioles won the World Series in 1966 and 1970.

Who hit the most home runs in his career?

Hank Aaron hit at least 20 homers in 20 seasons, smashing 755 in all. Although he never hit more than 47 in a season, he is still the greatest home-run hitter ever. Aaron topped Ruth's old record of 714 career home runs on April 8, 1974, while playing for the Atlanta Braves. It was one of baseball's greatest moments. "I purposely never smiled as I ran the bases after a home run, but I suppose I couldn't help it that time," Aaron wrote of his record-breaking shot.

Hank Aaron had a lot of chances to hit home runs. He played in 3,298 games during his 23-year career.

SMITHSONIAN LINK

See "Hammerin' Hank" Aaron's Milwaukee Brewers jersey, from the final 2 years of his 23-year career, at: http://americanhistory.si.edu/sports/exhibit/gamemakers/aaron/index.cfm

Which player hit the most home runs in a season?

Babe Ruth, "the Bambino," was baseball's first great home-run hitter. In 1919, Ruth set a record by hitting 29 home runs for the Boston Red Sox. A year later, playing for the New York Yankees, "the Sultan of Swat" set a new record with 54 dingers, and he swatted 59 the following season. Finally, in 1927, Ruth crushed 60 homers. That was the record for 34 years, until a quiet Yankees outfielder from Minnesota named Roger Maris shocked fans by hitting 61 in 1961. In 1998, Mark McGwire of the St. Louis Cardinals broke that record by slamming 70 home runs. Three years later, San Francisco Giants outfielder Barry Bonds set the new record when he smacked 73.

"I swing big, with everything I've got," Babe Ruth said. "I hit big or I miss big."

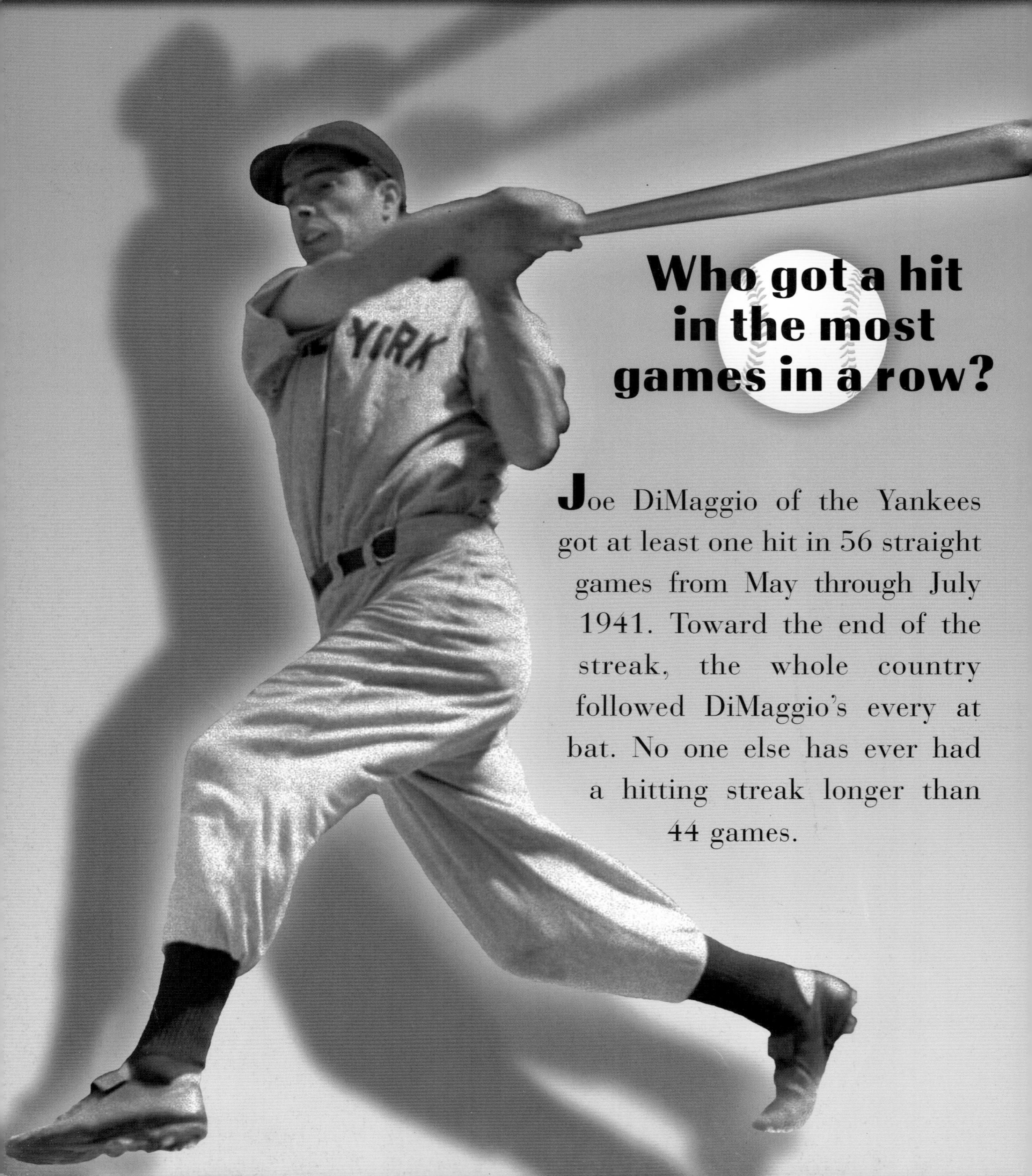

Who got a hit in the most games in a row?

Joe DiMaggio of the Yankees got at least one hit in 56 straight games from May through July 1941. Toward the end of the streak, the whole country followed DiMaggio's every at bat. No one else has ever had a hitting streak longer than 44 games.

Cal Ripken shook hands with Baltimore fans the night he topped Lou Gehrig's streak.

Who played the most games in a row?

Lou Gehrig played in 2,130 straight games from 1925 to 1939. But then Gehrig became ill and could no longer play. He suffered from a crippling illness people now call Lou Gehrig's disease. Few fans thought anyone would ever break Gehrig's record. Then Cal Ripken, Jr., of the Baltimore Orioles played in 2,632 straight games from 1982 to 1998. When Ripken took the field on September 6, 1995, to break Gehrig's record, it was one of baseball's most magical moments. Most fans are sure that Ripken's record will never be broken.

In 2004, Roger Clemens became the oldest pitcher ever to win the Cy Young Award. He was 42.

Which pitcher won the most games?

Twenty-two pitchers have won 300 games, but only Denton "Cy" Young won more than 500. Young won 511 games pitching for five teams from 1890 to 1911, but he also lost more games than anyone else, 316. Every season, each league gives a Cy Young Award to its best pitcher.

Roger "the Rocket" Clemens has won a record seven Cy Youngs.

Top 5 All-Time Win Leaders

PLAYER	W	L	ERA	SO
1. C. Young	511	316	2.63	2803
2. W. Johnson	417	279	2.17	3508
3. G. Alexander	373	208	2.56	2198
4. C. Mathewson	373	188	2.13	2502
5. J. Galvin	365	310	2.85	1807

* Statistics as of October 19, 2006

W = wins
L = losses
ERA = earned run average
SO = strikeouts

Top 5 All-Time Strikeout Leaders

PLAYER	W	L	ERA	SO
1. N. Ryan	324	292	3.19	5714
2. R. Clemens	348	178	3.10	4604
3. R. Johnson	280	147	3.22	4544
4. S. Carlton	329	244	3.22	4136
5. B. Blyleven	287	250	3.31	3701

* Statistics as of October 19, 2006

What was the longest game ever played?

The Chicago White Sox and Milwaukee Brewers started a game on the night of May 8, 1984, that didn't end until the next day. After 19 innings of a tie game, the teams went home and finished the game the next night. Finally, in the 25th inning, after eight hours and six minutes over two nights, Chicago won, 7–6, on a home run by Harold Baines. It was the longest game in major-league history.

Who pitched the most no-hitters?

To throw a no-hitter, a pitcher must complete a game without giving up a hit.

If a pitcher completes a game without any batter reaching base at all, it's called a perfect game.

The incredible Nolan Ryan, "the Ryan Express," threw a record seven no-hitters. Even more amazing, there were 18 years between his first no-hitter, in 1973, and his last, in 1991.

On May 1, 1991, Nolan Ryan struck out 16 Toronto Blue Jays during his seventh no-hitter.

Who struck out the most hitters in a single game?

Roger Clemens struck out 20 batters in a game twice while pitching for the Boston Red Sox, first in 1986 and again in 1996. Kerry Wood of the Chicago Cubs matched the feat on May 6, 1998. How great were these three pitching performances? Neither pitcher walked a single batter in any of them.

Kerry Wood gave up only one hit the day he struck out 20 Houston Astros.

Has anyone ever won a World Series by hitting a home run?

Every player dreams of coming to bat one day in the bottom of the ninth inning with a chance to win the World Series with a home run. Two players have actually done it. In the seventh and final game of the 1960 Series, Bill Mazeroski of the Pittsburgh Pirates launched a homer in the bottom of the ninth to shock the New York Yankees, 10–9. In 1993, Toronto Blue Jays outfielder Joe Carter hit a three-run homer to beat the Philadelphia Phillies and win the Series, four games to two. Both home runs are among the most dramatic moments in baseball history.

Bill Mazeroski hit his home run to win the 1960 World Series in front of the home fans in Pittsburgh.

Who won the first World Series?

In 1900, the seven-team American League challenged the older National League to a series between their champions. In 1903, the National League finally agreed, and the first World Series was on.

The leagues decided that the first team to win five out of nine games would be the champs, and the Boston Americans of the American League—today's Red Sox—beat the Pittsburgh Pirates, five games to three.

Has a pitcher ever thrown a perfect game in the World Series?

In the fifth game of the 1956 World Series, Don Larsen of the New York Yankees pitched to 27 Brooklyn Dodgers and got every single one of them out. The Yanks won the game, 2–0, and the Series, four games to three. **"They can never break my record. The best they can do is tie it,"** Larsen said.

Smithsonian

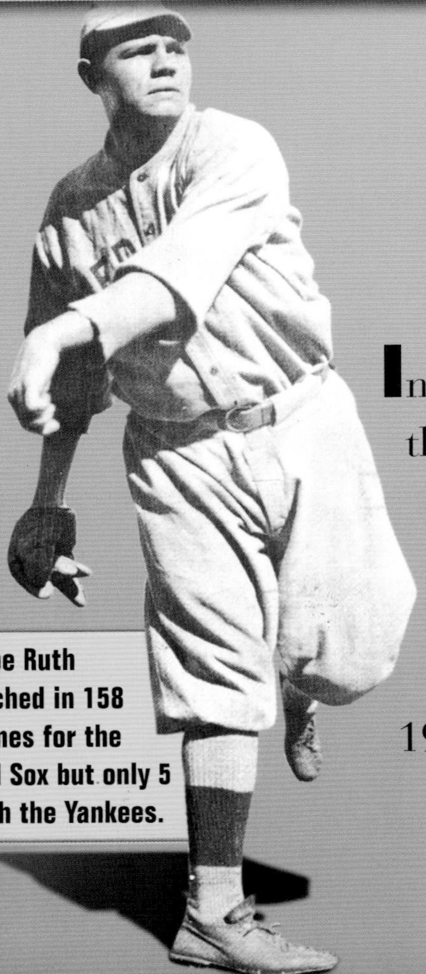

Which team has won the most World Series?

In 1919, the New York Yankees, who had never won the World Series, acquired the great pitcher and hitter Babe Ruth from the Boston Red Sox. That changed everything. With the Yankees, Ruth stopped pitching—but he never stopped hitting. He won four World Series with the Yankees (in 1923, 1927, 1928, and 1932).

Babe Ruth pitched in 158 games for the Red Sox but only 5 with the Yankees.

Today, the Yankees hold the record with 26 championships in all.

SMITHSONIAN LINK
Learn more about Babe Ruth's astonishing baseball career and view a ball he autographed in 1926 by going to:
http://americanhistory.si.edu/sports/exhibit/superstars/ruth/index.cfm

Lou Gehrig won the American League's Most Valuable Player award in 1927.

Who was Mr. October?

The Yankees have had many World Series heroes, but what Reggie Jackson did in the sixth game of the 1977 Series was something special. Jackson crushed home runs in three straight at bats, each time off a different pitcher, each time on the first pitch of the at bat. His home runs helped the Yankees beat the Los Angeles Dodgers, and Jackson lived up to his nickname, "Mr. October," for his postseason play.

The 1927 Yankees may have been the best team in baseball history. They won 110 games, scored almost 400 more runs than their opponents, and were World Series champions. Ruth hit 60 home runs, Lou Gehrig hit 47, and the entire lineup got the nickname "Murderers' Row" because they "killed" pitches.

Reggie Jackson hit five home runs in the 1977 World Series.

What is the All-Star Game?

Most fans dream about the teams they would put together if they could pick from all the superstars in both leagues. Once a year, they get that chance. Since 1933, baseball has taken a short break in the middle of the season for the All-Star Game. The game is played in a different ballpark each season. The starting players are chosen by the fans, who cast millions of votes for their favorite stars.

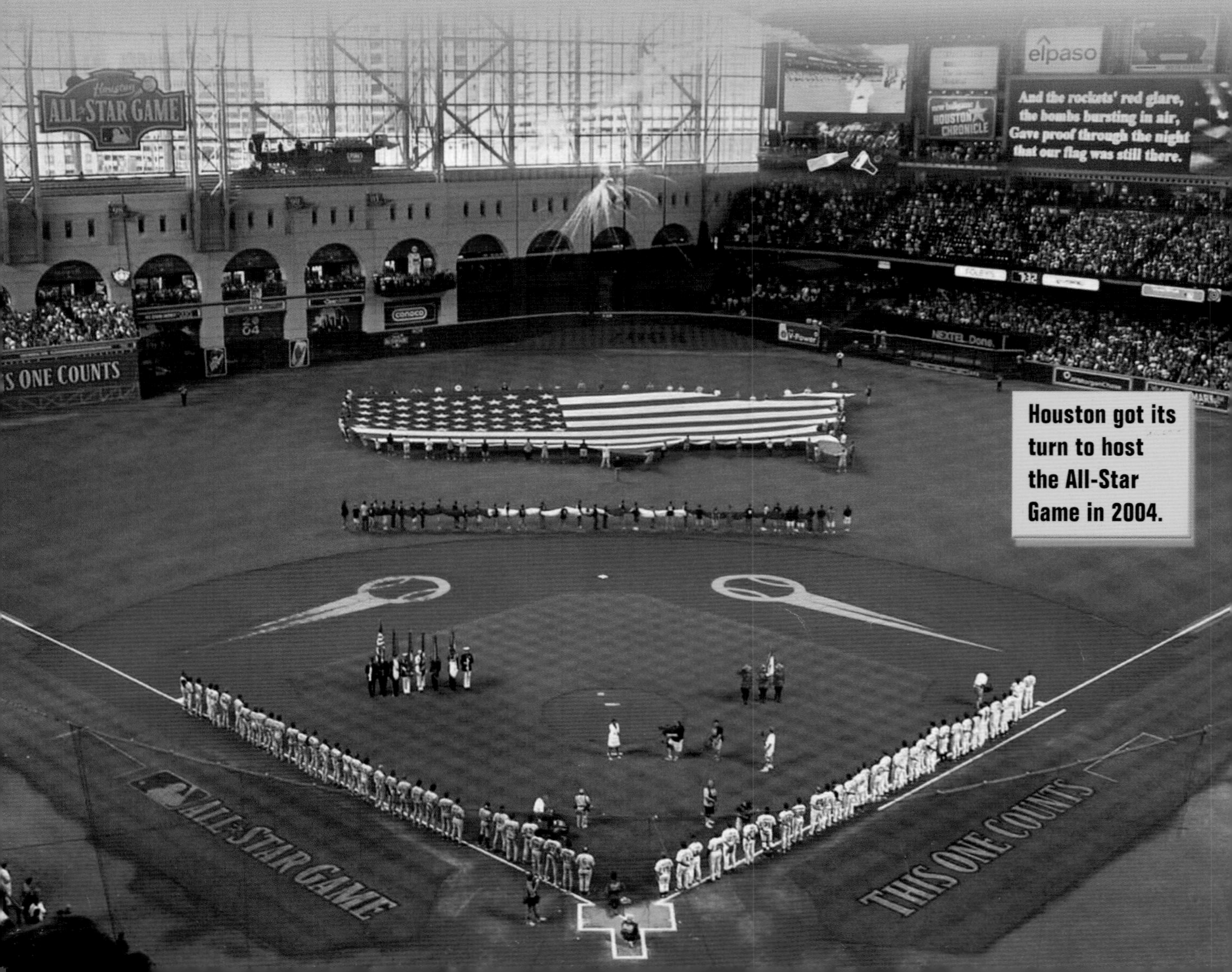

Houston got its turn to host the All-Star Game in 2004.

Who has played in the most All-Star Games?

Three players played in the All-Star Game 24 times—Stan Musial, Hank Aaron, and Willie Mays. Musial, the great St. Louis Cardinals left fielder, also hit six home runs in All-Star Games, more than anyone else.

Cardinals star Stan Musial [second from right] jokes with Willie Mays [right] at the 1956 All-Star Game.

SMITHSONIAN LINK
See the bat that St. Louis Cardinals outfielder Stan "the Man" Musial used to smack his 3,000th hit—a double on May 13, 1958, against the rival Chicago Cubs—by going to: http://americanhistory.si.edu/sports/exhibit/additional/index.cfm#

What are the greatest moments in All-Star Game history?

The great Babe Ruth hit the first-ever All-Star Game home run in 1933 to lead the American League to victory. In 1941, Ted Williams smacked a deep three-run homer in the bottom of the ninth to give the American League a 7–5 win. The 2002 All-Star Game in Milwaukee is one that many players would like to forget. As fans booed loudly, the game ended in a 7–7 tie after 11 innings, because both teams had used all their pitchers, and baseball rules do not allow players to return to a game once they have been taken out.

What were the Negro Leagues?

Satchel Paige gave his best pitches nicknames, like the "Bat Dodger."

Until 1947, African Americans were not allowed to play major-league baseball. So some of history's best ballplayers played in the separate Negro Leagues. The first league was formed by Andrew "Rube" Foster in 1920. Teams and leagues often changed, but some clubs, like the Kansas City Monarchs, the Indianapolis Clowns, and the Homestead Grays, were always popular with fans. The Grays, who played in Pittsburgh and Washington, D.C., may have been the most successful team. They won three Negro League World Series titles in the 1940s.

SMITHSONIAN LINK

See a Jackie Robinson trading card and photos, along with a baseball signed by the 1952 Brooklyn Dodgers, by going to: http://americanhistory.si.edu/sports/exhibit/firsts/robinson/index.cfm

Josh Gibson (standing, third from right) played in a Negro League All-Star Game in 1939.

Who was the first African American to play major- league baseball?

In 1947, Branch Rickey, the president of the Brooklyn Dodgers, decided it was time for African Americans to play in the majors. He chose Jackie Robinson to be the first. Robinson took the field for the Dodgers on April 15, 1947.

His career was difficult. Racist fans treated him badly. But Robinson kept playing, and he became one of the greatest second basemen of all time. Soon other Negro League stars, like Hank Aaron and Willie Mays, entered the major leagues. "I felt like if Jackie could do it, then he had given every black kid in America that little ray of hope that they could do it," Aaron said.

Jackie Robinson was a fearless base runner. He stole home base 19 times.

Who were the greatest Negro League players?

Grays' catcher Josh Gibson may have been the best home-run hitter ever; many fans believe he hit at least as many as Ruth and Aaron. James "Cool Papa" Bell was the fastest player in any league during the 1930s, and no one could hit Satchel Paige's fastball.

What was the All-American Girls Professional Baseball League?

In 1943, the United States was fighting in World War II. Many major-league players, like Ted Williams, left their teams to become soldiers.

Chicago Cubs owner Phillip Wrigley decided to start a women's baseball league to keep fans interested in the game. The All-American Girls Professional Baseball League had teams in several cities in the Midwest, and thousands of fans enjoyed the games. Before the league closed in 1954, more than 600 women had played big-league ball.

As a girl, Jean Faut practiced her pitching by throwing rocks at telephone poles.

In **1952**, major-league officials ruled that none of its teams could hire women players, and no team ever has.

SMITHSONIAN LINK

Betsy Jochum starred in the All-American Girls Professional Baseball League and won the 1944 batting title, earning herself the nickname "Sock'em Jochum."

See her South Bend Blue Sox uniform by going to:

http://americanhistory.si.edu/sports/exhibit/champions/jochum/index.cfm

Who were the league's greatest players?

Doris "Sammye" Sams of the Muskegon (Michigan) Lassies was a star pitcher and outfielder. She was named the league's Player of the Year in 1947 and 1949. In 1952, she set a league record by hitting 12 home runs.

Pitcher Jean Faut of the South Bend (Indiana) Blue Sox was Player of the Year in 1951 and 1953. She won 140 games in her career, lost only 64, and pitched two perfect games. Lavonne "Pepper" Paire was a catcher whose teams won three league championships. She also wrote the league's theme song.

Players from six AAGPBL teams pose for a group picture.

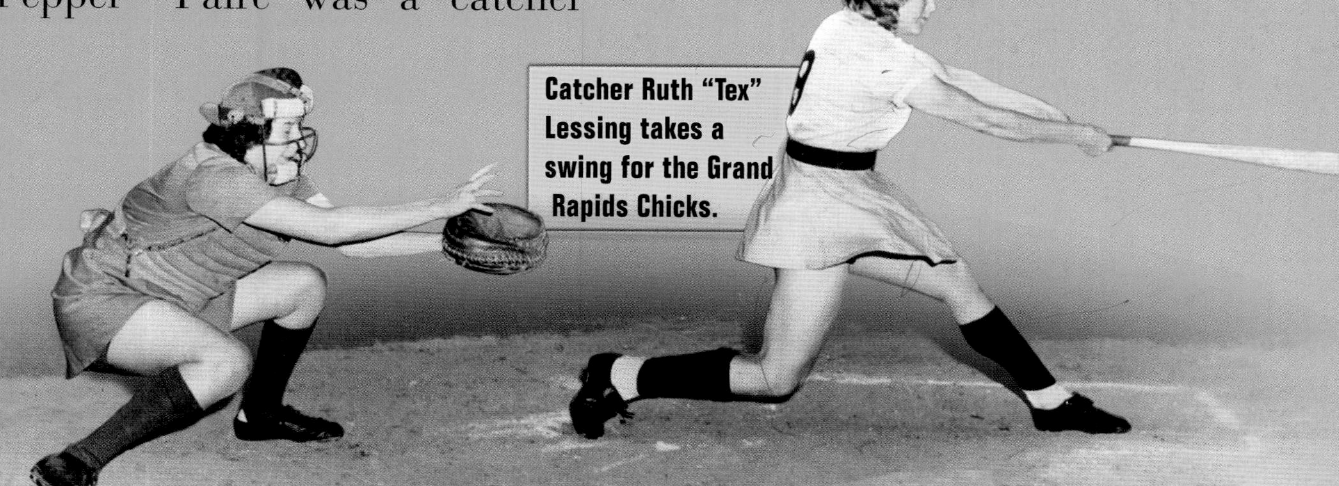

Catcher Ruth "Tex" Lessing takes a swing for the Grand Rapids Chicks.

350,000 people visit the
e in Cooperstown, New
year. Seeing each Hall
plaque is a highlight of
e museum.

What is the National Baseball Hall of Fame?

The National Baseball Hall of Fame and Museum honors baseball history—the game's greatest players, records, and games. Each year, the Baseball Writers Association of America votes to decide whether any retired players should become new members of the Hall of Fame. A player can be voted into the Hall of Fame after he has been retired for five years.

The first Hall of Famers were Ty Cobb, Babe Ruth, Honus Wagner, Christy Mathewson, and Walter Johnson. They were elected in 1936.

What can you find in the Hall of Fame?

The Hall of Fame is the country's biggest baseball museum. Visitors can see caps, uniforms, bats, and balls that were actually used by Hall of Fame players. The Hall also has exhibits about every part of baseball history, from great World Series games to record-setting feats and great moments from the Negro Leagues and the All-American Girls Professional Baseball League.

If you want to see Babe Ruth's locker, Nolan Ryan's spikes, or Jackie Robinson's jersey, they're all in the Hall.

In how many countries do people play professional baseball?

An American teacher at a school in Tokyo introduced Japanese students to the game in 1873. In the same year, miners visiting Australia taught baseball to people there. By the 1930s, both countries had professional clubs. Today, people in more than 100 countries play baseball.

In 1889, a group of American ballplayers visited Egypt, where they taught the game to Egyptians and visited the famous Sphinx.

In 2006, Japan won the first-ever World Baseball Classic, a tournament with teams from 16 countries.

St. Louis Cardinals star Albert Pujols was the National League MVP in 2005.

Which countries have the most players in the major leagues?

United States	590
Dominican Republic	85
Venezuela	43
Puerto Rico	33
Mexico	14
Canada	14
Japan	9
Cuba	6
Korea	5
Others	14

*According to 2006 Opening Day rosters (813 total players)

Who are the best players from around the world?

Some of the game's greatest players are Dominican, including sluggers such as Albert Pujols, Vladimir Guerrero, and David Ortiz and pitchers such as Pedro Martinez. Right fielder Ichiro Suzuki of Japan is one of the world's most exciting and popular players. In each of his first five seasons with the Seattle Mariners, he had more than 200 hits (including a major-league baseball record 262 in 2004), stole more than 30 bases, and made the All-Star team.

SMITHSONIAN LINK
Find out about the Puerto Rican baseball hero Roberto Clemente and see his actual batting helmet by visiting: http://americanhistory.si.edu/sports/exhibit/champions/clemente/index.cfm

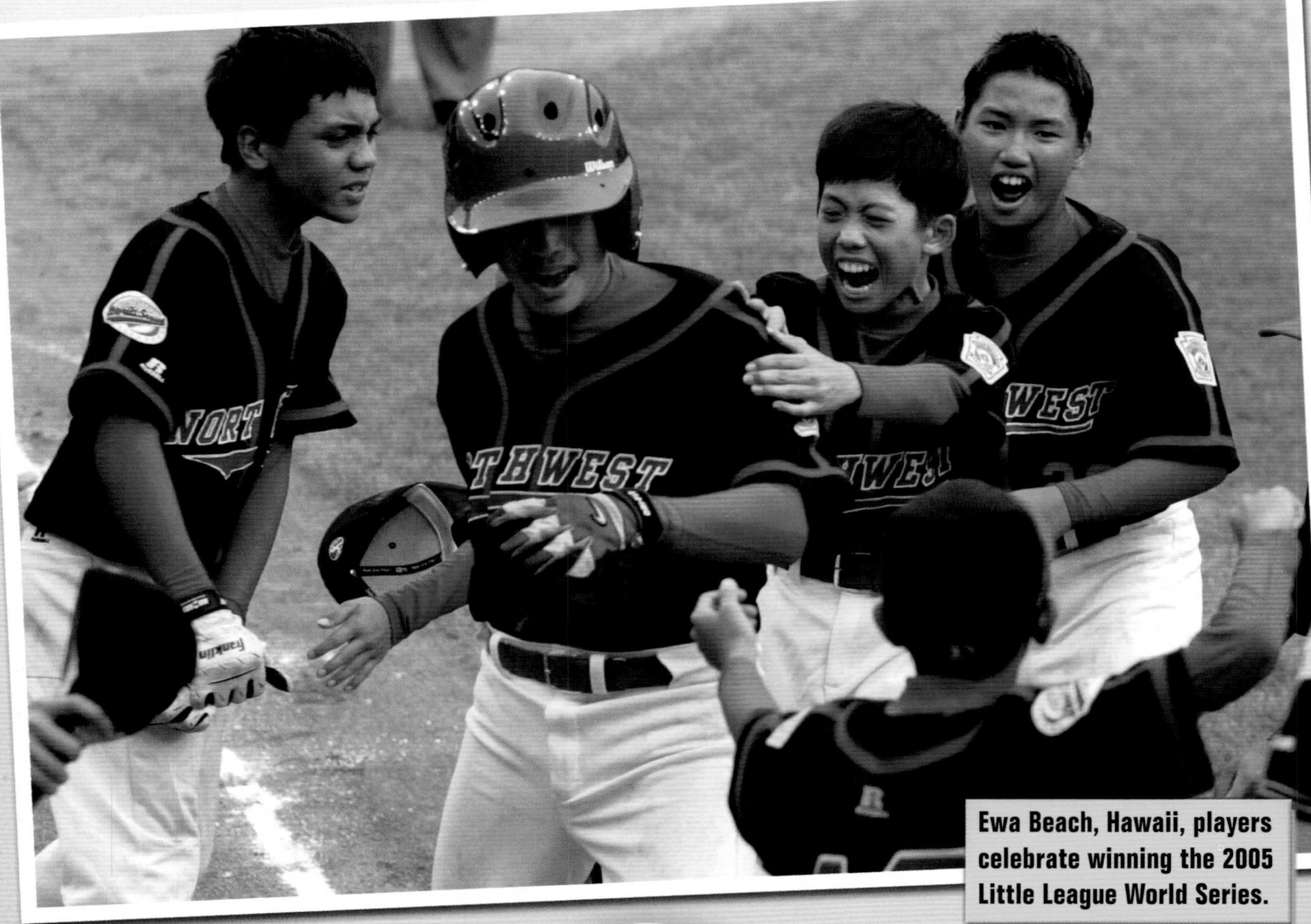

Ewa Beach, Hawaii, players celebrate winning the 2005 Little League World Series.

How long have kids played on Little League teams?

Children have played baseball in fields, sandlots, and streets since the game was invented. Little League Baseball began in 1939. Games last only six innings, and players use bats made of aluminum instead of wood.

Today, thousands of boys and girls play on organized Little League Baseball teams.

Is there a Little League World Series?

Each summer, teams from around the world come to South Williamsport, Pennsylvania, to play in the Little League World Series. All the players must be 11 or 12 years old. After 10 days of play, the best team from the United States plays one game against the best team from outside the country for the world title. Eleven players have played in both the Little League and major-league World Series, including big-league stars Gary Sheffield and Jason Varitek.

Have any Little Leaguers made it to the Hall of Fame?

Thirteen Little Leaguers have grown up to become members of the Hall of Fame. They include the great left-handed pitcher Steve Carlton, who struck out 4,136 batters; third baseman Mike Schmidt, who clubbed 548 home runs; and left fielder Carl Yastrzemski. "Yaz" was the last player to win baseball's Triple Crown for leading the league in home runs, batting average, and **runs batted in.** He did it in 1967.

Red Sox star Carl Yastrzemski played Little League ball in Bridgehampton, New York.

Ted Spencer
VICE PRESIDENT AND CHIEF CURATOR
NATIONAL BASEBALL HALL OF FAME

How did you become a curator at the Hall of Fame?

I actually started out in the design field. My college degree is in fine arts. I was working as a design manager when I saw an ad for the Curator of Exhibits at the Hall of Fame. As the museum grew and matured into a significant museum of American history, I grew with it.

Did anything or anyone from your childhood influence your decision?

When I was in the second grade, I would draw pictures of baseball games. I was also the bat-boy for my father's baseball team. I'm named after Ted Williams, so you can see that my parents are ardent Red Sox fans.

What is the most surprising thing you have learned about baseball?

The more I worked in our collections and archives, the more I came to realize how important The Game is to our history and culture. Baseball was called the "National Pastime" five years before the Civil War!

What do you enjoy most about the game?

The Game has been such a big part of my life. It brings back memories of being at games with my parents (briefly with my grandfather), later with my three children, watching my boys play, and now watching my grandson learn to throw and bat. The great strength of the game is how it connects generations.

What's your favorite team? Who's your favorite player?

Absolutely the Red Sox! As a child I seemed to root for the average players.

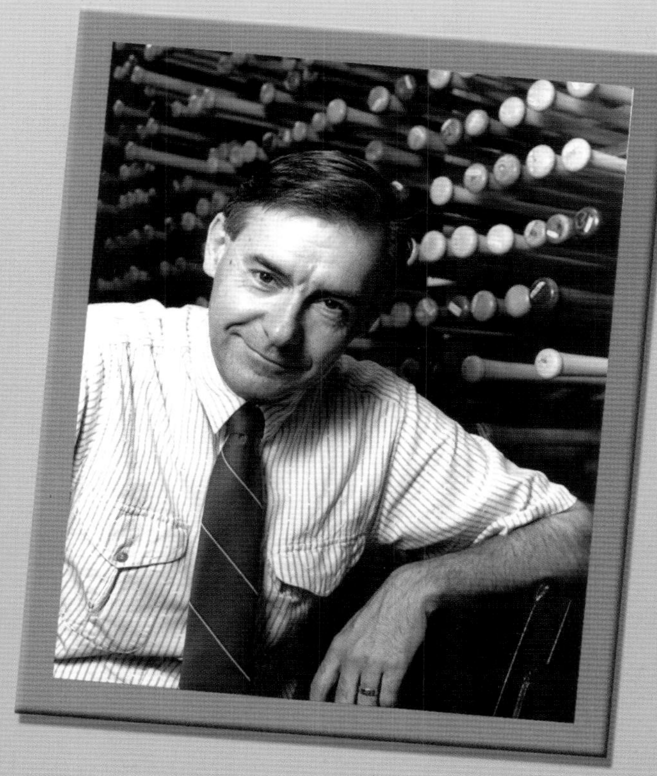

One I followed faithfully—even though he never played for the Sox—was Tito Francona. How ironic it was to see his son guide them to the 2004 World Championship. My favorite Red Sox were Ted Williams, Jim Lonborg, and Jim Rice.

Did you play the game when you were a kid?

I played four years of Little League in Quincy, Massachusetts, in the 1950s. But I never thought I was good enough to try out for my high school team. I wish now that I had at least tried.

What do you do on most days?

A typical day for a curator could mean delving into any historical aspect of the game. Sometimes it will be big, important and easy-to-find information on a Hall of Famer or the World Series, but sometimes it may be looking for one game, or event, involving an unknown ballplayer in the nineteenth century. That's really the most fun and rewarding.

Where and when do you do your research?

Almost all of our research is done within the Hall of Fame's library and collections vault.

What do you like most about your job?

Discovering information that I never knew before. Every day, while going through the archives, a curator can find something that has been forgotten about for decades or something that no one knew about at all.

What do you like least about your job?

Not enough time. Not enough space. There are so many aspects of The Game that are very important, but we don't have enough time to do the research needed and there is just not enough space in the museum to tell the story.

Baseball Terms

at bat—A player or team's turn to hit.

base hit—Another term for a hit. If a player reaches first base on a base hit, it's called a single; second base, a double; third base, a triple; and home plate, a home run.

bullpen—An area at a ballpark, often behind the outfield fence, where pitchers can warm up, or practice, before coming into the game.

doubleheader—Two games played by two teams against each other on the same day.

double play—When a team makes two outs on the same play. For example, if there's a runner at first base and the batter hits a ball to the shortstop, the fielder throws the ball to second base before the runner from first reaches it. Then the second baseman throws to first base before the batter reaches that base.

dugouts—Areas built into the ballpark, one on the third-base side, one on the first-base side, where players, managers, and coaches sit when they don't have to be on the field.

earned run—A run that scores that isn't the result of an error by the fielding team.

earned run average—The average number of earned runs per game scored against a pitcher; determined by dividing the total number of earned runs scored against him by the total number of innings pitched and then multiplying by nine.

extra innings—When a game is tied after nine innings, the teams play extra innings until one of them wins.

grand slam—A home run hit when there are already runners on first, second, and third base. A grand slam counts for four runs.

inning—One of nine periods of a regulation baseball game. Each team gets a turn at bat that is limited by three outs per inning.

rookie—A player in his first season in the major leagues. The American League and National League give Rookie of the Year Awards to their best first-year player every season.

run batted in (RBI)—When a batter gets a hit, a walk, a ground-out, a sacrifice fly, or a fielder's choice that allows a runner already on base to score, it's called a run batted in.

shutout—When a team keeps its opponent from scoring any runs in a game, it's called a shutout. When one pitcher gives up no runs in a complete game, he gets credit for a shutout.